NATURAL TAKEOVER OF SMALL THINGS

Camino del Sol

A Latina and Latino Literary Series

NATURAL TAKEOVER OF SMALL THINGS

TIM Z. HERNANDEZ

THE UNIVERSITY OF
ARIZONA PRESS

TUCSON

 THE UNIVERSITY OF ARIZONA PRESS

© 2013 Tim Z. Hernandez

www.uapress.arizona.edu

Library of Congress Cataloging-in-Publication Data
Hernandez, Tim Z.
Natural takeover of small things / Tim Z. Hernandez.
p. cm. – (Camino del sol: a Latina and Latino literary series)
ISBN 978-0-8165-3012-0 (pbk. : acid-free paper)
I. Title.
PS3608.E768N38 2012
811.6–dc23
                2012027712

Publication of this book is made possible in part by the proceeds of a permanent endowment cre-
ated with the assistance of a Challenge Grant from the National Endowment for the Humanities,
a federal agency.

Manufactured in the United States of America on acid-free, archival-quality paper containing a
minimum of 30% post-consumer waste and processed chlorine free.

18   17   16   15   14   13   6   5   4   3   2   1

For Rumi, Salvador, and Quetzani, so that you cannot forget

CONTENTS

I. Arms Up In Dead Heat

II. San Joaquin Sutra   27

III. Natural Takeover of Small Things

NATURAL TAKEOVER OF SMALL THINGS

Surrounded by bone, surrounded by cells,
by rings, by rings of hell, by hair, surrounded by
air-is-a-thing . . .
—**Jack Collom,** *Ecology*

Yo no soy guajiro, ni campesino/
pero entiendo esta tierra a través de su ritmo . . .
—**40 Watt Hype**

In poetry everything is permitted.
—**Nicanor Parra**

ARMS UP IN DEAD HEAT

HOME

Fresno is the inexhaustible nerve
in the twitching leg of a dog
three hours after being smashed
beneath the retread wheel
of a tomato truck en route to
a packing house that was raided
by the feds just days before the harvest,
in which tractors were employed
to make do where the vacancy
of bodies could not, as they ran out
into the oncoming traffic of Highway 99,
arms up in dead heat, shouting
the names of their children,
who were huddled nearby,
in an elementary school, reciting
out loud, *The House That Jack Built.*

THE TRUTH ABOUT SMALL TOWNS

Mistral was dead wrong about small towns.
She must've been referring only to that cathedral
in Santiago, Chile, or to her own mother's habit
of saving crippled pigeons trembling near
a marble fountain. For had she seen the way
Tejano mothers clutch cut garden hoses in east
Orange Cove, or how the blackbirds taunt the weeping
wires down from telephone posts at dawn,
she might have put things differently—
She might have instead wrote, small towns are caught up
in a lust for domination. Someone builds a silo,
someone tears it down. Someone impregnates the child,
another leaves it in the bed of a truck for someone
they never met. Even the train tracks end here, and serve
no purpose, except to house a single jackrabbit, content
on procreating with its shadow. There certainly would have
been no mention of lullabies after witnessing how wheat,
felled by a freeze, still manages to whisper abhorrently
about its offspring.

BROWN CHRIST

Yesterday, I saw God,
a brown Christ hovering
above an onion field
over tilled plains of the San Joaquin—
frayed constellation of denim,
ox hide work boot broken at the heel,
a curved knife gripped in his fingers,
low clouds undulating, hair of broken
lemongrass & rodeo lasso,
a fragrant beard of perejíl,
everything smelled of sulphur
& manure, the silos wept
and snowflakes tumbled tenderly
from the day moon, refracting
luminous congregations of aspen,
with the music of truck dogs
howling over accordions,
shimmering manna-light.

OLD SCHOOL

The neighbors crop of weed is abundant,
and who knows why the church across the street
cannot smell skunk skewering the liturgy, or why
the nearby library has not filed away complaints
to the sheriff's department, or how the cops and paramedics
did not discover it last time they were called to the house
for a beating that took place at two in the morning,
in the front yard, when Bonafied, the pitbull, had a taste
for the mistress's thigh meat. From the sidewalk,
through cracked lips, *Darnel! Do your wife know*
you fucked me this morning! Until wife tore out
the screen door, and the kids laughed from bedroom windows,
stoned from sleep, siren lights and cell phone frequencies
lifted up, with the old school music of flesh on flesh, falling
over the other, guttural heaves from beneath
womb shots, spinning like a dusty record warped from decades
of heat, skipping over the beat, until it sounded like
the point had been made.

TWO GIRLS

From my kitchen window
I see the trailer park

where two little girls
crouch and pee against

a diamond link fence.
How easily they squat

beneath the umbrella of their skirts
paying no attention to the magpies

perched in the trees
or the squirrel's parasitic carcass

stewing in the hot dirt
near crushed beer cans

yellowed from a fire
the night before. No concern

for the man in the window frame
who regards himself as a poet

and smothers two slices of wheat toast
with sautéed spinach leaves for breakfast

because gone are the days

when the top button of his pants was still intact.

How simple those times

when one could expose their thighs

to pee beneath the open eye of sky

and not fear what lies beyond the fence.

THE DAY JOHNNY TAPIA DIED ON MY SIDEWALK

was the same as yesterday. A cart crammed
with Mexican pastries, a man beneath a blue umbrella
calling out, *Mayonesa!* Out front the barren lawn,
the pitbull chained to fence post, lapping its testicles
and griping at the sun.

The church bell rang and the school bell rang.
Both bells rang in concentric circles that rose up and skimmed
the bellies of the departing planes that disrupted
the satellite discs over the houses sagging on Kenmore Drive,
where girls in tight jeans walked hand in hand with boys
in tighter jeans. Krylon-sprayed ball caps cocked to studded
ear lobe, sideburns trimmed to a blade.

Across the street, McLane High was pep rallying
to the instrumentation of brass and skin, while worn
stadium lights spilled dimly down Clinton Avenue.
The football team was dressed and counting down
the kick-off. The weed-eater buzzed next door.
On the front porch children practiced dance moves to a pop
tune, outdated. Across the street, campesinos bumped
Ramon Ayala's early days, about a corner in the sky, snapped
open cold bottles of X on the driveway, still arguing
over who was more Mexican than the other.

FORECLOSURE BLUES

You can keep the plaster walls, undulating
shadows, holes in the yard, sunk garden,
dead rat sleeping on the front porch, blue jay
feathers blown over the brown grass, bullet hole
in tornado fence, where tired balloon casings
sag by metallic string, cabinet doors missing,
camphor tree triplets dropping bronze leaves,
stucco and siding stripped, stored amid the Night Jasmine,
shingles bunched like raisins, and single pane
windows without locks, hardwood floors that bark
when stepped on, the children's room painted
with flowers and sweet things, a coil of butterflies
fades, while the mail slot is silent, the lamp knows
it can't be left behind, the numbers on the curb
have ran off with the last rain, the stove's jaw won't close,
the pigeons are plotting, and if you find the cat keep it,
but let the calla lily bulbs sleep, out of sight, as they will
come to learn of the foreclosure on their own.

BORN INTO IT

Gravel necked pluckers
of elephant hearts, collapsed
ladders, calluses like hardpan,
short-handled hoes, to him
and her and they, the soil is
second nature. He enters into
worry daily, and leaves
drunk with prayer. She has seen
the violet burn off in bonfires
and smudgestacks rise again
by morning. What invisible defeats
have they swallowed that the unending
sentence of their dream flows
from the mouth like an aqueduct,
in which the water has been
siphoned and fish now constitute
the last stand?

HISPANIC UPWARD MOBILITY

Before he left the grapes for good.

Before he bequeathed his curved knife to the junkbox indefinitely.

Before he traded flannel for rayon, sweat-rag for necktie.

Before he went ultraviolet to a/c.

Before he switched from back roads to highway.

Before he pulled his savings from the mattress and used the word 401k.

The metamorphosis was frightening.

So, immediately he fucked the first white secretary

within reach, and then called a mandatory staff meeting

to discuss the ins and outs of fiscal responsibility.

HE APPEARS

hungover after last night's rage,
come filling up this throat, this eye
and mouth, this living room,
the sagged curtains and tiny
eyeballs set in their sockets,
corrugated from heavy rains,
a hailstorm, and the beaded necklace
that separated across the hardwood
floor, and once again he dislocates
a joint in the body, to where the spine
touches its own tip, and slowly, with slight
calculation, the head tilts and makes
a face like a grape five days
into sunlight.

EL GRITO

Sunday again,
in the back of a van,
behind *El Siete Mares,*
the voice yawned
before climbing into her
suit of lights, her pressed bolero,
buttons bowed before
the horn arrived, glassy
from last night, and then el requinto
with a dirty rosette, strapless
but fine-tuned, the violin spat
and adjusted her girdle, primped
her bow in rosin, shit-talkin'
those who ran late, until
el guitarrón, breathing heavily
from behind his tonsils,
crammed himself into the van,
shut all doors, and sent around
a broken clarinet reed,
loaded with coke.

SALINAS AS A SUCCULENT

While driving to Dinuba
I saw you, Omar, squatting
like a doomed succulent
in those fallow Sanger fields,
communing with crow
and night crawlers, whispering giddily
about the happy hour
of a new reservoir
opening up on the east side,
where once stood
El Monterrey Bar
with its off-key accordion
and saggy breasted women
slopping suds from
warm Schlitz.

Yes, it was you offering up
a used napkin stained with pastrami,
muttering lines from an old movie
starring Steve McQueen,
and when that didn't work
you organized the ants
to haul off a felled oak leaf
that threatened its allegiance
to the queen, until the seagulls
arrived fresh from the dump-yard,
in manta whites, so you left, hell-bent
on crashing the all-night party
of gardenias.

DEAR HECTOR,

The old campesino died today. He wasn't ready, I could tell.
I had been with him the whole week. Flew in from Denver
on a Sunday red-eye and went straight to the hospital.
He was sitting up and talking like his usual self.
Except that his teeth were missing. But his appetite
was still there. On Monday afternoon he asked me
to get him a sandwich from the Oval. Said the hospital
food was killing him, claimed he could taste Atrazine
in the lettuce. By Tuesday, he stopped walking.
Just sat up in his bed, scratching his face and wondering
where the hell I'd been these last few months. I told him
school. He asked me if I brought my video camera along,
and I said I did. He had some things to say. By Wednesday
he was laid out. I had to prop his chest up with pillows
during the filming. He spoke about mundane things,
but it all seemed important to him. A dishrag he had left
on the kitchen sink. The lawnmower that belonged to the
neighbor. Mousie and her puppies under the front porch.
Aunt Hilda, the most filial. He worried for her. Even remembered
a grocery list in his pants pocket. Asked me to get it, so I did.
Asked me to read the items that had yet to be scratched off.
Butter. Pimiento. Moyejas. And then a card for Hector, my son.
He was too tired to sign it, Tomorrow, he said. So we left it
for tomorrow, which is now today.

UNDELIVERED POSTCARDS TO LYDIA

I don't want to see you now or ever in monsoon pesadilla
anchored to plasma tendrils & radiation, tumble-weed
stricken between old Socorro & injected skins of the San Joaquin.
I never wanted these things for you—
la pisca on a never-ending vine, stretching the horizon,
to a sagging army barrack in Korea, your father blowing
Woody Guthrie in harmonic shrapnel sandwiches, discharged
for government cheese and bad piñones, while the bouganvillea
eavesdrops on the windowsill, pretending not to listen.

I am here now, on the shadow side of the Rocky Mountains,
weighted by papers, contemplating the soft tooth
of a wolf spider hunkered in the sycamore, perched on the banks
of a rivulet, until I can no longer decipher the beats
of my own breath, from the intoxication of unnamed insects
sexing in the fragrant willow.

Lydia, I have heard that there are cemeteries in Socorro
where headstones are kept clean by iguanas with tiny fingers,
whose tongues are immune to the scorpion's sting.

Socorro!

Where you found your sister in a methamphetamine dream,
later to hallucinate ghetto birds in Bakersfield boneyards.

Socorro!

Where neutron bombs blossom over the Sandia Mountains,
and molecules are still recovering from the eternal blush
of deafening red.

Socorro!

What have I left out? Boyle Heights? Dinuba? A left breast?
The Great Horned Owl hunkered in the sycamore?

What does it matter?
In the end they will say, Lydia.
Who throws lamps at her children and tames them
with broomsticks. Lydia who wails for barefoot babies with dirty faces.
Little Lydia with her brother's jeans. Lydia of Deming, New Mexico.
Lydia of Romo. Of East Los Angeles. And of the gardens
in the suburbs. They will say Lydia who dropped out. Lydia who married
the gangster. Lydia with the white face and thin lips, who swears
by astrology but doesn't tell God. Lydia with the harvested lymph nodes.
Lydia bowing in the groves. Lydia in an open field of alfalfa.
Lydia whose eyes turn auburn in sunlight. Lydia who mothers
other people's children. Lydia with a gift of listening.
Lydia with a gift for you. They will say Lydia was my mother. That Lydia,
the woman who was paranoid about the end. Lydia who had a book

written in her head. Lydia whose son took the kids and fled. Lydia with biceps like warm dough. Lydia who kept Birds-of-Paradise on the kitchen table. Lydia who delighted in old avocados in bread. Lydia whose epitaph will read: Just don't forget me. There goes Lydia they will say, I was lucky to have been held by her.

MY NAME IS HERNANDEZ

It means descendent of Hernan Cortez.

Said Spaniard, who slayed Moctezuma
            and a nation of ore,
occupied the territories

known since as Southwest. Enslaved captives
            who stewed in venomous marshes of mud and thicket,
forced to shoulder slabs of glass shard obsidian,

pummel the soft gold wading in unknown depths
            drown for the nugget
tear tule from the root, mule the rotund

mounds of clay up mountain crags, named for Gods
            with uncollected debts,
to shape indestructible pylons of new empire rising.

—Though I am not this dramatic by any means.
I watch television in my boxer shorts,
eat sardines from the can, breathe on my children's faces

just to watch them shriek.

My name is Hernandez.
            My father is a fieldworker. Every sugar beet
you've ever eaten he's shorn away what threatened to destroy it.

When I was born he wore me on his back
            while slouching over a short-handled hoe
in the monsoon plains of five Wyoming summers.

There is too much time for memory to be accurate.
My father's worked since the day of his conception.
A shoe-shine boy in the parlors of south Tejas.

The adobe tiles were relics
from days of indentured servitude. Earthen red
clay shingles the boy destroyed with rifle.

Mesquite is what he recalls mostly.
And how the chicharra's song is a quantum thread
between this life and that.

I see him now, behind the wheel of a rig,
hazardous materials, head a snow-capped
slab of insidious worry. Illuminated by the coo

of a grandson,
the most fragile ammonite coiled in the shape
of his own quavering hand.

*

My name is Hernandez.
Born of a woman who was born of a woman . . .
though I've said this once before.
Don't let her flexible disposition fool you. Consider the blade of a palm leaf,
on Palm Sunday.
Consider the Sabbath, Ash Wednesday.
She is devoted to the countdown
of years, starting from ten. Her time here is limited.
Same is true for the rest of us.
Except she has gotten good at forgetting this.
We haven't.
We miss. She lets on a permanence, not seen since
the resurrection.

*

My name is Hernandez.
Of a Dinuba Sanitarium that crumbled in '89.

Of an elementary school hidden between a plum orchard
                    and the voluptuous golden thigh of a foothill.
Of an education that included the neon powder of sulfur.

Of menial jobs—fast-food dives and an auto detailing stint.
                    Of thirty days in the Tulare County Jail,
and then five more.

Of flea markets and strip malls.
                    Of television 'round the clock.
Of relationships to things and people that rarely go the distance.

Of constantly risking solitude.
                    Of the grandfather on Magnolia Way,
who pickles eggs in a tin shed behind a sulking house with two mortgages.

Of the twin abortions.
                    Of regrets.
Of saying things like regret because it's expected.

Of reneging on words.
                    Of doctoring the wounds with words.
Of admitting he knows nothing of words.

*

Years ago, while living in South San Francisco, I walked into a Carniceria
                    with my last name emblazoned on the window.
A young man draped in a blood apron greeted me.

I ordered three tacos de lengua, and smiling
                    I told him that I was a Hernandez too.
Yes, he replied.

Handing me the change.

          Dicing the cow's last word on the cutting block, he said,
There are millions of us here.

Millions of Hernandez's.
          Each one
expecting some kind of deal.

After Martín Espada

II

SAN JOAQUIN SUTRA

Valley of Saints;

> where holy preachers and Night Train drunk vagrants
>> hobble their limbs in Oval Park,

where once Lincoln's beard got served

> the wasted pulpo of seven seas

> and the people lit up dazzling lights on Christmas Eve,
>> where in mud ditches

bathe the nude brown children

> & broken whites

> who together learned to speak crawdad
>> in irrigation pipes,

> barefoot on busted wine bottles,

>> and when days extend their radiant arms
>> they follow the river into the mouth
>> and there again
>> learn to become mountain-child

> bulked like trunks of redwood trees,

where campesino grandfathers bait little ones
> with raw serrano peppers
> teaching them early

to memorize flavors of pain

> how the eyes flood, and the tongue is left
>> to burn in silence,

where tractor stoned youth chuck dirt clots at the testicles of bovines
> just to watch them giddyup their asses

>> in frightening masks, toppling the massive beasts
> from their heavy hooves,

>> guzzling gunpowder in bulge tight
>> denims and ostrich-hide roach killers

laughing at the cosmos lyric
in the radio box beaming
satellite signals across Scorpio's crab hands,
out among the celestial
expansion of the widest brim yet,
where stands a jail cell for every son, two for paroled transients
who sleep along drought stricken streams
beneath totemic overpasses
xylophone of ribs

ballad for bread
kneeling in shadows of Dairyland factories and packing sheds
that reek of bruised fruit,
mutiny bourgeoning   among the cashews.

I was there
in the vicious freeze of '98
wearing eggplant colognes & indestructible trousers,
stationed beneath burning oil heaters,
fanning the night with my holy hands
when salt rock bullets entered the flesh
and I experienced the first death—

Sacred valley of Kawhean rivers,
crooked horse legs creeked in crimson,
valley of thigh and crotch,
sacred lake of tule foliage
fossiled in conch shells and holy stalagmite,
—everything here sacred, you see
the ditch banks and mass choirs alike,
pious families and albino-eyed field mice
snarling at the sky,

            the foxtails and abandoned dogs of the countryside
                    wagging tongues

                                in dead air,

            sacred mariachi girth
            and carp scales lost in teeth,
            finger plucking catgut,
        smooth river   rock and fungal gutters
                and neon waters trickling in the chasm,
            sacred the young mothers and fathers—that never were
                the black moon of a mechanic's fingernail,
    the silos and chicken factories,
                        thick-boned and deplumed,
        sacred plumes of gagging monoxides
                            eclipsing azure,
    Elephant Heart Plums, sacred,
                compost, compote, cotton gnats, sacred too,
                guns plunged through car windows,
                        the windows,
                            shards of color,
                    streetlamps in all directions, sacred,
    Impalas dragging tail
            in metallic flake saffron
                    airbrush burn Popocaptepetl
                            rebozo flowing lava

sacred,
trailer parks and horseshoes,
            spent condoms, the blood on the carpet,
    bottlecaps hammered on trunks of trees,
            abandoned carousels,
                stereos pulsing in the throat,
sacred.

The second death:

        Came from a tower of papier-mâché

        amid the sneering eyes of the projects

           and frigid TV dinners,

barren bus stops and unemployment lines,

        a phalanx of reapers armed with golden shields

        issued by the public in ballot boxes

          and rigged elections,

    a nickel-plated bullet piercing

        drab doorways into half-dead hearts of men

—only considered men on tax returns and obituary columns,

        and by the women who swill beer at their expense,

and then a wristwatch heirloom from an old man to his grandson,

      desert turquoise in the eyes of molded silver,

        South Texas gypsy campesino,

   a halo of breath escaping the body,

and then a chair weaver

  from the mountains of Nuevo Léon,

      painter of strange lotteries,

        a devil's tender spear, stairwells leading

        nowhere—

who I once saw suck

  the god end

of a cactus spike

  and hallucinate Yeshua

rainbows above the highway

  where deadly manures stir

      in the pearl center of table grapes

       tucked in a cove along the bountiful foot

        of the Sierra Nevadas—

Erasmo!

 I say your name and hear the clarion wails

   of a thousand egrets lofted in the willows like upturned tears

waiting to drop

Erasmo, where are your chairs now?

     In what cave do you find yourself, sulking acrylic

abstractions in the dark? Erasmo—who sleeps in the melancholic sag

of a hammock and waits

     for the company of an abandoned accordion

       smashing Mexican pulp

        in the blinding guajillo seed

          of sunrise.

       Saint Gabriel;

       B-ball dreamer,

       lost in rural tendril of vine and barbed wire and late night

          taco truck

          philosophies.

What of Buche?

     How it glistens vulnerable with the sensuality of a tender throat.

How the Lengua?

     Offering hymns to congregations with deaf ears.

Why tripas?

      Mad holy cow with incest in the skull,

      we celebrate your return with sacrifices and pyres

      smoldering in the stomachs

      of empty tin drums

      somewhere in the hearts

      of narrow towns tucked

amid tilled soil and tract houses
and the vanishing plots of empty dirt
where man has yet to break ground.
San Gabriel;
patron saint of discarded dreams,
hear the cry of new voices suffering
in methamphetamine fields,
where crouch the stillborn
harvesting stoned crutches
and bleeding karmic livers
that run and pollute the unearthed mineral of drink.

Valley of strip malls and manure,
glittering drags of cocaine and hydraulic chariots
that creep the dusk trail of moons & onyx pathways,
where Friday night drive-thrus and panting liquor stores
hustle north face with the same evangelical promise
of prescribed medicines
that jolt the Southside Wives Club
into misshaped injections and unnatural jawlines
—noses in the china cabinet!
San Joaquin Valley,
where tired faces water quaint gardens with cut hoses,
bending to bury
the corn next to the sugarcane, reaching
for the avocado on the highest branch,
the melon's elusive fragrance
in all directions toward all the windows in all the houses on all the streets,
sweet invisible nectars   drifting
in vastness of big sky
where taunts a   kite

                    broken   free

    of its

                                                strings.

                              ✦

        St. Jack
of the holy waters,
            why have you split your aqueducts
like you split your lover's legs,
            and chastity-cemented her fertile ravines?
And now the trout aspire for wings
            and each day awaken with the lust to fly
            among the swallowtails and catapult Devil's Ridge
fluttering gills among the white majesty of solar fans
            down into the peninsula,
            where fled generations before generations
that returned defeated and aged,
            gambling their luck on offspring
                and dueling religions.

                              ✦

    I sing the praises of the campos,
            the pale trains and panaderos baking sweet bread
                before Venus's bashful face vanishes in the fold of night,
    and the worker vans hum engines and stutter into sunrise,
            the campos where dirty-faced infants

crawl among swept gravel and jump rope
                  escapularios blessed in DDT showers,
         campos like poorly sewn seams on the ragged end of a skirt
            flittering on invisible zephyrs
         living prophetic corridos
               on the nylon strings of a splintering vihuela,
campos in the ghostly architecture of dissolved Chinatowns
        across the tracks   from the Sports Arena,
where line the glistening gutters with erect meters and expiring clocks,
   where behind the Kearny Fish Market jezebels cop nasty paychecks
        & spend the day drunk on dumpster juices,
campos of Ararat, where stirs the inconsolable gait of The Avenger's eyes
           lurking among the poppies, gun smoke unfurling
   loose fogs of Yettem,
          and the campos of Oaxaca
         who speak wrecked dialects of Mixtec,
         pawing piña against a wail of dueling tubas,
             and the campos of Portugal and Cambodia,
              hovels of cornstalk and bamboo—

Internment everywhere!
Internment in the cherry blossoms and whispering magnolia—
Internments of jade and alabaster drowned in silk—
Internments on Houston & N.E. 4th Street,
     where mohawkcholadykes ball gangbangers
initiated under Belmont St. black lights,
        and down low councilmen
bask in golden showers, bugling Bull Elk speak
        to the hustling gargoyles of ghetto Zoos—
Chukchansi internments!
Mono chump change rattling powwow horse prayers

at the methadone clinic—

Internments of aborted fetuses and undocumented brassieres

pinned to clotheslines

wavering for a breast—

Middle-class interning students with immigrant tongues

and five-fingered candles

lit 'round the clock—

Yokohama blurring Oklahoma dust,

calligraphic internments scrawled

with brass Heron beak & feathers of mud,

unmarked codices translate the demolition,

Laos and the Philippines

—elsewhere.

San Joaquin—

where sickly bodies of old Texan mothers draped in aprons of sunflower

and waning seasons sit idly by, waiting for some slick cancer to escort

their last days to proms of disintegration, while the souls of

amputated limbs

twitch anxious habits for workloads of the waiting day,

and the cemeteries crowned in tornado fences, warped from the weight

of age, keep porch poets and lesser known names, scrawled in Krylon

hieroglyph over barbed boughs and broken pipes, cemeteries huddled

in shadows of obese mortar castles that have impregnated the land

with palm trees

where no such trees exist.

San Joaquin Valley, why are your back roads stricken with altars,
and your plastic carnations entombed among deflated balloons?
What keeps the tattered photographs from disintegrating with the dew?
Who dies in the back of a narrow van,
limbs splayed to the heavens?
Who survives?
Who arrives first?
Who will harvest the bodies?
Who will recall them in a dream?
How does one return the belongings?
When names fade where do they go?
What Country will claim the purgatoried?
What is the geography of hell?
Who inherits the wreckage?
How deep the ravine of a child's memory?
Are there two sides to the swallowtail's account?
What business has the worm entering the persimmon?
What galaxies in the mollusk?
Whose bell in the pelvis?
Do crucifixes exclude?
What irrigation of blood?
Does a fig weep in the open air?
Does water discriminate?
What of sirens?
How do we count the invisible?
Can angels scale border walls?
Who will open the gates for them?
Who denies them?
What manner of love is this?

III

NATURAL TAKEOVER OF SMALL THINGS

NATURAL TAKEOVER OF SMALL THINGS

How can I tell you that I know nothing
about migrations, though there are pieces of me
left in the chamber of a Glock 35
from back in the day, when I adhered
to the mystical uncertainty of gutters?

How can I tell you that I have worked no land
but the copious things I've grown unintentionally;
like facial hair, or morning breath, or one more
habit I will grow old with?

How can I tell you that when I first bit into a Fuyu
persimmon, dusk tasted this way, the afternoon
my grandfather died—a thick wedge of air, sweetened
by an emptiness?

The more I tell you I am not, the more I am convinced
that the eyespot of a peacock's plume stares, knowing
it will later in the right hands become the object
of some misspent lust, or a tassel on the rearview mirror
of an abandoned Chevy pickup truck on the outskirts,
surrendering its wheels to sediment, bequeathing its engine
to the natural takeover of small things.

ON THE CORNER OF CEDAR & CLINTON

I notice sodden balls of cotton left flattened in the mud after the storm

I notice toothless fences

I notice the lazy morning bus lines drooling down Cedar Avenue

I notice the bubbling throats of pigeons hunkered in the headwind

I notice the telephone wires listening

I notice a feral dog whimpering in the oleander

I notice the difference between car engines

I notice a child pointing up and calling out, *clouds!*

I notice the fermented stink of windfallen oranges dead in hot sun

I notice a stillborn left with cleft palette

I notice an orgy of flies sexing atop a pile of horse shit on the shoulder

I notice train tracks end here

I notice cantaloupe halves that make women blush

I notice all seventy-eight varieties of lemon yellow

I notice peach fuzz burns

I notice collateral genitalia

I notice knock-off chains made from recycled ammo

I notice the dead fog on the front lawn

I notice the warm rat at the back porch

I notice pollo rostizado smoke tethered to a market on Tulare Street

I notice the house half without electricity

I notice the morning fight over bills

I notice her voice like a rototiller

I notice the chemical log spitting in the fireplace

I notice the significance of roman numerals spray-painted on broken fences

I notice the short illuminated flight of dust

I notice abbreviated moustaches in line at the liquor store

I notice transparent brassieres taunting in the laundry pile

I notice the arcane nature of txt mssgs

I notice a polite conversation between two mosquitoes on my hand

I notice the soles of my feet when they're naked

I notice the heartbeat inside my throat when I am out of breath

I notice the wet eyes of girls brawling in alleyways behind the House of Pho

I notice delicate measurements in the jagged line of a tired face

I notice contradictions like hunger amid the breadbasket

I notice the holiest of flights in a crow carcass

I notice death in these lines, and in your lines too

I notice life in the autumnal glow of a Meyer lemon

I notice the song of possibility seeping in a fallow field

I notice life in rocks, and felled trees, and embers

I notice life mostly when it does nothing but ignore you

I notice the raw truth inherent in words like "rocks" and "raw"

I notice when I am about to notice something mostly unnoticeable

      like micro-movements

         or the end of an orange

           or how the horizon at dawn rarely goes the distance

I notice words like "anger" do something to the gut

I notice the gut and torso and limbs notice their own things

I notice the color green in gutters and in leaves

I notice life in a leaf

I notice a leaf fallen to the asphalt

I notice the sun in the fallen leaf—on the asphalt

I notice there is no death, only sun in a fallen leaf

I notice the lack of sky too

I notice the fragrance of night jasmine *before* night

I notice daylight in shadows and dilated nebulas in the pupils

I notice one big populous moving to an incessant drum without dancing

THE TRACTORS

They came growling their
   cylindrical teeth,   rabid,
      gunning for the   ripest
         cherry between   virgin
            foothills swelling   toxic
               sunrise and   dirt,
                  red enough to   recall
                     the last   slaughter

They came   tilling
     in tongues   unrecognizable
       a sliver of   fingernail
         cutting into   sediment,
           a tool to   disembowel,
             ammonite   uncoiled
               at the   root,
                 a margin of   water
                   tickling, bony   claw

They came   horny
     in metallic   drag,
       multiplying, a lustful   pack
         of dogs lapping up the   buzzard's
           remains,   excavating
          the sodden   flesh
            of the Choinumne   people,
              who still   preside
               in the red   eye
                 of an almond   blossom

They came flexing their   make
        assembled from bumpers and   axles
                and from the water   mark
                of short handled   hoes,
                        they measure their   worth
                                in hectares and interim   flows
                                        judged, and   devoted
                                                to the silvery   sound
                                                                of   fluid

INSTRUCTIONS FOR THE ALTAR

Once I have slipped from my skin into sediment

amid salted alluvials

gathering east of the Rockies

or among the sagging algodón

defeated by valley fog

in preparing the altar

follow these instructions:

I have no regrets

therefore no water is necessary

for dim ablutions,

rather, let the dirtiness of smoke

recall the unpredictability of my name

When I awoke, I did so knowingly

I have never been afraid of the dark,

yet, when I shut my eyes

the invisible becomes apparent

There are no heavens where heavens await,

   no pyramid but in the sternum,

only angels and corrupt deities now;

Release the sage from its bundle,

   the scapulary too

Release the tooth of a snowflake
　　from its own sudden drift

To what water does the arroyo submit?

Release the gnarled bough in holy books

Release this name
and all that it conjures;
not the kiss or penetration,
not the naïve boy whistling by the ditch-bank
somewhere on an obscure hillside,
or the father's tenderness
moment after moment;

I see you standing against
the dull saffron of a Western sun
and think of how one enters the world headlong,
devoted to the flesh,
born majestic,
bloodied & writhing,
no mind prayers concocted—

　　　　　　origin of prayer
　　　　　　someplace else

　　　　　　　　　　　　origin of plum blossom
　　　　　　　　　　　　one beat before the scent

　　　origin of suffering
　　　various hells occur simultaneously

origin of Juan Diego
a fruit stand south of Delano

origin of Nirvana
ass flat burnt from too much now

origin of The Kingdom
tenderness of the heart

origin of Samsara
consistently returning

origin de Fé
si Diosito quiere

origin of Ahimsa
a teardrop tattoo

origin of Allah
prostration of kisses

origin of Olé
Allah caught in the act

If after these preparations
I still have yet to return
then do as we discussed
that one slow night over a six pack
& bagful of spent pistachio seeds,
about how you wouldn't search for me

in lush blue cemeteries,
about how you wouldn't pray for me
    at magnolia shrines every Day of the Dead,
about the emptiness of an altar
    and the tiny flickering candle
    above the golden chalice
    that rests atop your collarbone,
instead, make offerings to the blessed
    calling of impermanent gut
—move on.

EIGHT SHOTS OF OVAL PARK

Cryptic glyph
skirls Pawn Shop
window where man leans
into a totem of television
screens reflecting

Krylon piss
on the warped dumpster
that sits like an obese woman
in front of Ofelia's Tacos
confined to a wheelchair
made of cardboard
& cancerous tin
cans of malt cobras
hissing

Watch dogs
on invisible leashes
yap jowls & slaver
over shaved ice
that melts and becomes
a trail of ghosts
rising up from cracks
in the drought of sudden

Thai boys
w/ busted laces
tongues torn
out burn
earnings in placard
elegies of blue

Beneath bondo fenders
& neon trucks
with cocks 'n' carousels
the hood hides
a mouthful of engine
idling

Chris's Meat Market
with gutted parking meters
ripped open curbside
brown glass
mixing with the green
the transparent
to be found

Shoeless Hmong women
hunkered in the faded

awning, hush the bellow

of trumpet & qeej

serenading the corn

woman in the dark kiosk

straw brooms

usher in the moon

Nine red steps

of St. Mary's Church

crumbled

covered in nettles & clippings

scuffed streaks

in the atrium

Joseph with his nose

chopped off

pigeon shit

on the marquee

a message:

FLYING PARALLEL

While driving home from work this evening
a hawk flew parallel to my window.
In its talons a baby squirrel tousled,
its wide black eyes alert to its situation
as the ground fell beneath.

Another bird, smaller in size,
came to the squirrel's rescue, pecking the head
and back of the hawk, parallel to my window.

The squirrel's tail spun, as if a disengaged
propeller ascending between two cliffs.
On one side the crags of sure death.
On the other, a small glimpse of what it
means to be reborn.

Parallel to my window, there were three lives
mid-flight, each of them arguing about their differences.
None of them prepared to let go.

STILL LIFE OF MENUDO WITH MORNING NEWS

Sunday morning

after the party

head fattened

w/ blood & booze

grind oregano

between palms

emerald spike of perfume

the scent of dirty green

a gothic flora/ Fallujah

flakes of crushed pepper

drifting the honeycomb

busted ristras

bombs above Los Alamos

behind the teeth

radiant esophagus blossom

belly fat & porous

pig foot

slop of wet earth

cartilage rich

sal y limón

citrus dawn

in South Valley grove

methane soup

tink of spoon on ceramic

gut music

harp & ham-hock

happening

slurp

hominy blue

harmony of seed y metate

calcified caracol

white cebolla

sugar & succotash

drought flowering

volcanic root grind

truncated cilantro

sprig pissing phosphor

auroras in cotton

hung drunk & starved

tasting nothing.

DEATH MEDITATIONS

I

Take for instance this body
16.07142857142857 stones of it
hair tufts in crevice
two moles in the crease of the neck
implanted seed of coriander
veins teal in tomatillo
skin that hides viscera,
observe closely the shape
of bone across the hand
the ankle supple, white
like aspen, how the stomach bulge
makes room for the lung
filled with air, take
for example a perfect row of teeth
the umber sun set in the center
of two eyes, the lips curl
run the tongue over plum
flesh of mouth, consider
how you know this
impossible aroma
enter the nose this way
imagine the cilia
leading to blood
where do rivulets make a home inside you?
watch the hairline wane

into tide of skull

when the moon rises

disintegration sings

watch tenderly at how the follicle bows

and lifts from the root

and catches flame

steal breaths from yourself

replace the lungs with rubble and fertilizer

listen to how the cells clamor and burst

layers of flesh peel like paper in bonfire

everything ashen and released

gaseous fissures

crackle and whistle, pungent

stink escapes the body

gelatinous marrows stew in the bone

consider your own decomposition

what questions will remain

stirring in the life-warm

wraith of memory?

II

As if a single blossoming

orchid bomb

drops scattering pistils

across the narrow lane

I swerve in floodlights

dodge engines that drop

from clouds thunderous

monsoon against the soft

xeriscape blue sage

and lavender burning
oil and lament among
the rows of children scowl
beneath the smudgestack's torch
I reach back to touch
my daughter and she is nowhere
in her car seat a wad
of baby clothes velcro shoes
tumble out from a hole
in the floorboard
and I've forgotten again
to remind myself to breathe

III
Sit among the aspen
anywhere in the Sangre de Cristo's
sometime in mid-October
and witness beautiful death
red and livid, releasing
its grip like a campesino's
golden severed hand reaching
for the buried beet of earth,
or the last migration
of brass butterflies flailing
wings against the tenderness
of space

MANTRA CHORES

Dogs without leashes/ hyacinth needs no watering/ boil water for
noodles/ wear the same clothes to bed/ as the night before/ a walk to
the mailbox is too far/ a drink of water/ is drink of cosmosis/ cocoa
is a mysterious bean/ my daughter tugs at her ears now and then/
the morning starts cool then heats up/ the clouds pass and clear/ I'm
hungry then I'm not/ gasoline is the price of it/ my wife brings me/
one egg over easy/ we hardly eat together anymore/ ponder water/
incestuous religion/ the computer holds up/ I haven't bought new
clothes in over two years/ every day comes with a sacrifice/ traffic
awaits/ so do dishes/ & children/ photos need eyes/ a staff meeting
at noon/ showers wash away dirt/ it should be so easy/ ambition
stresses/ relaxation comes natural/ all things natural as they are/
soap/ carpet/ the shyest star/ every window with its view/ of some
destruction/ a door is hung/ when last was the hinge oiled?/ music
is fixed/ betabel as beat/ downtrodden is a hill/ from the other-side/
the incline/ atmosphere is akashic/ constellations gossip/ old is new
backward/ back is old new words/ dying again/ from the beginning/
impossible simplicity/ pious trends/ street fashion firmament/ book
ends/ unpredictable blood/ nerve ends/ transmitters of unspoken/
helix language/ impossible DNA/ unpredictable body/ unpredictable
ideas of body/ predictable unpredictability/ empty wallet/ filled
eyeglasses/ scuffed/ drink from sight/ hydration as vision/ the
mailman leads me to believe/ fork tines on teeth/ jícama on química/
perceived definitions/ of familia/ merciless nostalgia/ crayola gardens/
alphabet with protruding nose/ ink pen think/ evolving décor/ a
breath of fresh breath/ hunger is infinite/ speak means little/ gong as
art deco/ xeriscape Jesus/ false stillness/ idolatry as I/ slip on shoes/
import importance/ important paper/ still just paper/ wrinkle-free
fabric/ nebulae probing/ news as action/ measurable silence/ tap water
dancer/ consolidation loans/ con solid koan/ life by measurement/
alternative/ native altar/ beautiful pitiful/ signs/ keys/ zoos/ voiceover
poetry/ perfumed toilet paper/ pre-packaged chicken/ un-housed
human/ go figure/ prior tees/ pre-heated warming/ edible compost/
finite ideas/ words/ words/ as things to be done.

IF NOTHING ELSE

Naturally, you are concerned with the war on flesh
and the tank's pursuit of eardrums, the silent coupe stirring
in the nostrils, ammonia & lime erasing the damage—

Let me relay the wingspan of albatross curling over
the San Andreas fault line, where oil cranes peck black
plasma off ocean's back—

We have been searching for answers in a levitation
of creased khakis, liquor store gods swilling elegiac booze,
puddling asphalt for the departed, homeboy marrow
fertilizing flora of broken towns, barrios & skies without—

Here it is:
If nothing else, pay attention to the molotov
bouquet, flowering in the fist, waiting for a time like you—

After Banksy

TWENTY-SIX STARLINGS

I was twelve when I shot each one.
Didn't think twice. Pulled the trigger.
Lined the bodies up across the hot concrete.
It was a triple digit summer. With fork
and pocket knife gutted each one deliciously.
Torso to neck. Plucked gray eyes like seeds.
Splayed their entrails out to dry. Investigated
carcass. Scrutinized the supple head. Strummed
the fragile sternum. Pecked at the wings.
Searched hard for the secrets they carry.
Until my mother found me. In feathers and blood.
Didn't say a word. Didn't have to. She stood
enraptured. And the birds, flayed open uniformly.
As if calling from their still murmuration.

THE MYTH OF KORA

Kalimba was left between Gong and statuette; Jesus splayed on a rock.
My brass is old, spoke Gong, wide chime full of sorrow. Reverberation
is a myth. I tell lies to my children about a time that never existed,
they ask me for a story and I recite limericks, infused with songs of the
disparate. I was given a cushion once, and I sat, waiting foolishly,
like an object with purpose.

Kalimba chimed in; I feel your lament, Brother. Look at me, void of gut
& bone. From a fallen baobab I was born, prodded with spike and nail,
plucked on the shoulder of a road, insects poured out, monsoon of sound—
Hear my tines? Zimbabwe on a zephyr. None can touch the softness of
thunder where cavernous awaits.

It was a game, interrupted Jesus, a little thing called emptiness. See this
ring of thorns? A garden becoming. One stick for the laughable horizon,
the other toward the satellite's heart. This rock? An idea of erosion's pull.
Between two mountains, the space where music is born.

COOKED TONGUE

When it's hot it's most alive,
a bubbling stew-pot lisp
of hissing death in translation
atop the gas fire past
in the electric broiler mind
ripped to shards
in sulking cucinas of Florentine
cubed twixt nostalgic wad
of dirty yellow maize
sown in tule swamps of Aztlán or
the Afrikaans errata field
where tribes war in the parenthesis
like dueling spiks in gutter glyph
margins of east central Fresno
where bullhorns of bullfrogs croak and lick
the night clean of insects
and misplaced accents
cocked in loaded chambers
of mouth, tonsil, bell
all nostalgic lungs sigh
when steam sweats window and ceiling
and glands swell to taste
that unmistakable tinge
of sweetened blood
warming on the stutter
of a word becoming.

AS IF WE DIDN'T KNOW

that fetal death too
could be performed
by the workings of crop dust
impregnating space
with anti-jizm
stirred in the loins
of a laboratory cock-
tail delivered by appliqué
to the foreskins of sons
who have labored among
the stone fruit doula's
open
venous
blossom.

ADIOS, FRESNO

You could use more letters of love.
        Here, take these. You owe me nothing, except back pay.
    But I won't mention it again.
          Trust me when I say I'll have no regrets leaving you.
     Sure, I'll hear it from the homebodies
         and deadpan hearts, who were born, loathe,
         and beg to die
            amid the drugged poppies.

You can keep your fields, the sun will follow me.

      I won't reconsider.
        I've overstayed my welcome
          by three generations.

The musicians will be alright,
    by which I mean incomparable,
      by which I mean they get the work done.
A g-string hangs over the baseball stadium on opening night
        when the *whores* go two-for-a-buck
    beneath the peeling paint of homerun alley.

          Fresno, your mosques are waning
       and your restaurant kitchens are wetter
           than before.

Even the hungry are gutting cows in the pasture now.

The farmers buy their vegetables in supermarkets, you know?

There is a difference between lost and Laos.

One day you will have all the water you need.

Your statue of David of Sassoon could use a rest, Fresno.

Don't bother looking for me.
     I will be lost to myself for the next hundred cycles,
          on a mountain near Red Feather Lakes.
     Caught up in raising three children who won't mistake
          the humming of bees
          for their own ambition.

Fresno, I can see your underwear through the holes in your jeans.

     If I wanted to be politically correct I would have
          registered my vehicle.

I won't miss the pretense,
     or the way your midnight reeks of pissed yeast and salami.
I might miss the smell of a Huele de Noche during baseball season.
     Or the cut grass at Shazade Field.
          —damn, you're playing to my nostalgia again.
     It's all you're good for.

I'm glad you and I never had children.
There would've been this thing of blood between us.
          Don't get sappy on me.

     Outside the truckers are grinding their axles,
          and the exhaust pipes got the bulldogs going next door.

You look pitiful when you're in love.
          I didn't say beautiful.
This drought suits you.
     Am I being too hard? You'll get over it.
     The refrigerator almost burnt down the house
          last night and I kept thinking somehow
          you were responsible for it.

     The bullet hole in my fence can only stare so long.

My cousin Art is in rehab now, but the silos

                                                wont shut up.
The landscape talks the loudest shit in summer.

                        Fresno, you try too hard.

                Why'd you have to take Andrés Montoya from us?

        Fresno, I might return if you promise to be good.
Just that I can't stand the heat.
                There are too many I-can't-stands.
                                        As many fruit stands.
                My mind is a packinghouse
                                        with a sagging conveyor belt.

Strawberries should taste so tart.

                        Oranges should fit in the palm of an adult hand.

There's no such thing as windfall.

                        A Pluot is incest at its finest.

                                        Enough said, Fresno.

        Adios.

ACKNOWLEDGMENTS

Thank you to the following people for offering their support during the period it took to complete this manuscript: Junior Burke, Steven Taylor, Ed Ochester, Amy Gerstler, Tim Liu, and Major Jackson. Also, thank you to the California Center for the Book and Poets & Writers Inc. for consistently backing my play. For the community of writers across the San Joaquin Valley, a deep bow goes to the Hmong American Writers Circle, The Normal School crew, the Inner Ear Poetry spot, Ms. Mayo's Soulflower Productions, Sol's Casa de Poesia, Lee and Lisa's guest room, Pakatelas Radio on KFCF 88.1 FM, Random Writers Workshop, and Redwood High's Artist's Café. And for the crews and musicos who have performed many of these poems with me; Carlos Rodriguez, Richard Juarez, Tony Delfino, Alejo Delgado, David Herrera, Dayanna Sevilla, Marissa Rodriguez, Lance Canales, Aaron Wall, Andrew Martinez, Conjunto Califas, and Jeremy Hofer.

Some of these poems have been previously published in the following: *Wet: A Journal of Proper Bathing* (University of Miami), *The Devil's Punchbowl: A Cultural and Geographic Map of California* (Red Hen Press), *Black Renaissance Noire* (New York University), *In the Grove* (In the Grove Press), *The Kumquat* (University of California, Merced), *Highway 99: A Literary Journey*, 2nd ed. (Heyday Books), *Square 1* (University of Colorado), *Symposium* (Baobab Tree Press), *Uncontained: Writers and Photographers in the Garden and the Margins* (Baksun Books), *The Undercurrent, Border Senses, Infinity Journal*, and *Huizache*.

ABOUT THE AUTHOR

Tim Z. Hernandez is a poet, novelist, and performance artist whose awards include the 2006 American Book Award, the 2010 Premio Aztlán Prize in Fiction, and the James Duval Phelan Award from the San Francisco Foundation. His poems and stories have appeared in numerous anthologies and journals, and his books have been widely acclaimed, including a spot on NPR's *All Things Considered*. In 2011 the Poetry Society of America named him one of sixteen New American Poets. He holds a BA from Naropa University and an MFA from Bennington College and currently calls the Rocky Mountains home.